11,287

J
646.21
C

Corrigan, Barbara
I love to sew

I LOVE TO SEW

I LOVE TO SEW

Barbara Corrigan

DOUBLEDAY & COMPANY, INC., GARDEN CITY, NEW YORK

Library of Congress Cataloging in Publication Data

Corrigan, Barbara, 1922–

  I love to sew.

  SUMMARY: *Describes basic hand and machine sewing techniques with in-structions for making such items as belts, wrap-around skirts, curtains, and dolls' clothes.*

  1. Sewing—Juvenile literature.   [1. Sewing] I. Title.
TT712.C65   646.2′1
ISBN 0-385-03089-4 Trade
ISBN 0-385-03163-7 Prebound
Library of Congress Catalog Card Number 73–15333

Affectionately dedicated to

Bonnie, Celeste, Cheryle,
Chris, Darlene, Debbie,
Dede, Donna, Doralee,
Elise, Ellen, Geraldine,
Ginny, Gretchen, Jackie,
Jane, Jeanne, Julie,
Karen, Kathy, Lainie,
Linda, Liz, Lori,
Lynette, Marie, Martha,
Mary, Mary Ann, Marybeth,
Maureen, Missy, Pam,
Richelle, Ruthie, Sarah,
Sharlene, Shelly, Susan,
Tammy, Tina, and Vickie

CONTENTS

INTRODUCTION

In our great-grandmothers' time, little girls were taught to sew by making samplers, using a variety of embroidery stitches to form pictures and mottoes.

In those days children were not allowed to question the authority of parents, but we can imagine that being forced to spend many hours over such painstaking needlework must have caused a good deal of boredom, resentment, and frustration.

But as we all know, a skill acquired through a genuine interest and enthusiasm for the subject will be remembered longer and can be a source of great enjoyment for years to come.

Children really do love to sew, and what they enjoy most is to feel that they are accomplishing something that can be seen right away. The first comment on starting a new item: "Do you think I'll finish this today?"

There is little patience with long-term projects. They want to make something to wear right away, or gifts for parents or younger brothers and sisters. The joy and confidence of a child who announces "I made it myself!" is wonderful to see, and helps to make up for a few crooked seams and crude stitches. Perfection will come later!

This book does not try to advance any educational theories, but is based on my experience in teaching youngsters from age nine through the teens. I have found that it is best not to try to have them make things from commercial patterns before the age of twelve or thirteen. They are just not mature enough to understand the principles involved in a pattern. You can patiently guide them one step at a time, but they won't really understand the reasons for what they are doing, or remember how to do it another time. After about the age of thirteen, however, the necessary mental and manual co-ordination seems to develop quickly and naturally.

This book will deal mainly with things that can be made by nine to twelve year olds, though older kids enjoy making these things too, and will not need so much help.

Teachers, scout leaders, summer camp, or church youth leaders can organize groups to sew together. Kids enjoy a certain amount of competition among themselves, and yet they can be encouraged to express themselves without the constant pressure for good marks, or fear of failure, that they may have in their regular school classes.

A hint to busy mothers: A group of young friends and neighbors could be organized into a summer sewing group, perhaps with two or three mothers taking turns with the teaching. This can be a happy answer to "What can I do now?" especially on those long rainy days that so often spoil summer plans.

I LOVE TO SEW

CHAPTER ONE

GETTING STARTED

A NOTE FOR ADULTS:

Most homes probably have the basic tools needed for sewing. It is important, even for children, that the equipment should be of a good quality. Dull scissors and rusty pins can be very discouraging.

Most of the projects described in this book require only small amounts of material, and anyone who sews usually has vast amounts of scraps, which are ideal.

Youngsters are usually fascinated with the sewing machine. Press a button and out comes a new dress, without benefit of human hands or brain! This idea must be gently but firmly discouraged. Some hand work is always necessary, and it is important to develop the sort of manual dexterity that can only come from a great deal of practice with hand tools.

Basic sewing equipment:

Needles—an assortment of sizes 5 to 10 sharps; also a large yarn needle for embroidery.

Pins—good-quality sharp ones, called dressmaker pins.

A *pin cushion*—after you have dropped a box of pins on the floor a few times, you will see the reason for this!

Scissors—bent-handle dressmaker shears are best for most work—the 7-inch size fits small hands best.

Small pointed scissors are also useful.

A *thimble* to fit the middle finger of your sewing hand—and *please* learn to use it!

A *seam ripper*—this will get a lot of use!

Thread—size 50 mercerized cotton, in black, white, and assorted colors.

Tailor's chalk in assorted colors.

Ruler and *tape measure*.

A *sewing machine*—if this is kept properly oiled and cleaned, it will stand a surprising amount of abuse.

The first thing you must learn is to thread a needle and tie a knot in the thread. Cut off a piece of thread, about 2

Fig. 1

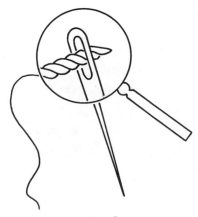

Fig. 2

to 2½ feet long, at an angle (Fig. 1), and put the cut end through the eye of the needle (Fig. 2). Moistening the thread with your lips (though not absolutely sanitary) makes the job easier.

Now make a knot in the end that was put through the needle eye. (The thread will tangle less if you always keep it running in the direction that it came off the spool.) Make the knot by following the three steps in Fig. 3.

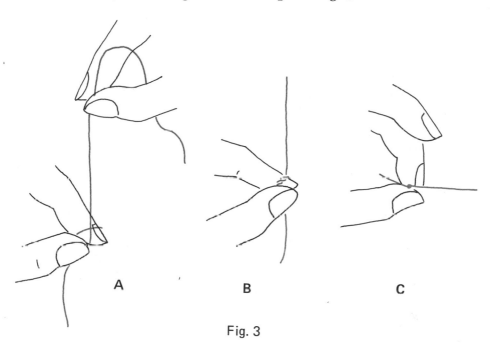

A   B   C

Fig. 3

Cross the thread over your forefinger, pulling the end up tightly with the other hand, and roll the thread forward with your thumb. As the knot slips off, grasp it with your thumb and middle finger until it is pulled up tight. Practice this—it should finally become so easy that you can do it with your eyes shut.

There are a few hand stitches that you will need to know. Practice these on scrap cloth before you start your first project.

Running stitch—the plainest stitch, made by putting your needle in and out of the material in a straight line (draw a chalk line to follow).

If right-handed, hold the cloth in your left hand, as in Fig. 4. Hold the needle in your right hand, with the thimble on your middle finger, ready to push the needle.

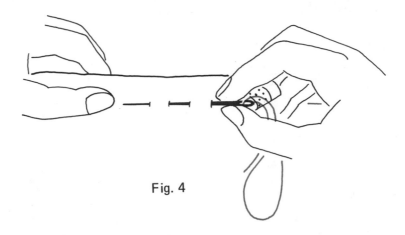

Fig. 4

You may take one stitch at a time, but with practice you can take several stitches on the needle, then pull them through all at once.

This stitch can be made very small, for finished work (Fig. 5).

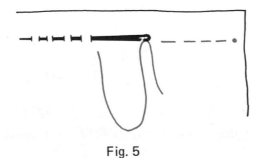

Fig. 5

The same thing done with longer, more widely spaced stitches, is called *basting* (Fig. 6), and is used to hold parts of your project together temporarily until the final stitching can be done.

Fig. 6

Backstitch—a stronger stitch for permanent work. Take one forward stitch, then a short stitch to the back of it (working right to left if you are right-handed). For each stitch, put the needle back to the end of the previous stitch, then bring it forward one stitch length ahead (Fig. 7). This makes a solid row of stitching on the front, with overlapping stitches on the back.

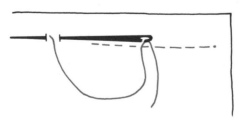

Fig. 7

Hemming—this basic slip stitch will do nicely for most hems. (And *no*, you do *not* stitch a hem on the machine, in most cases. It is not supposed to show on the right side of your work.)

Start by pressing under ¼ inch on the edge of the material. Then turn up the hem the desired width, measuring and pinning it every few inches (Fig. 8).

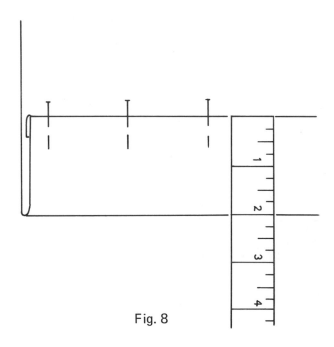

Fig. 8

Hold the material over your left forefinger (if right-handed) as in Fig. 9, and take one stitch under the hem fold to hide the knot. Take one small stitch directly below the fold, then slide the needle under the folded edge about ½ inch ahead, and pull it through. Keep the stitches quite loose.

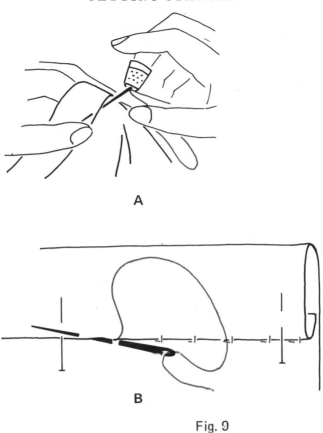

A

B

Fig. 9

Overcasting this is used for finishing rough edges, as a decoration for an edge, or for closing up stuffed toys and pillows (Fig. 10).

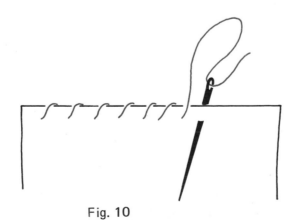

Fig. 10

Work from left to right, putting your needle in at the back of the material. Keep the thread up above the work to avoid tangling. Practice by drawing a chalk line near the edge to keep the stitches an even distance from the edge.

At the end of a row of any kind of hand sewing, you must fasten off the thread to keep it from pulling out. Take three or four small stitches all in the same place (Fig. 11).

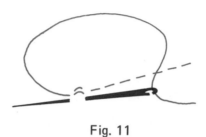

Fig. 11

The sewing machine. Now we come to the fun part! You will love using the sewing machine. Most children do—even boys.

There are so many brands of machines, all with little differences, that it is not possible to give complete directions here. Every machine comes with an operator's manual—a little book that tells everything about it—so before you start, have your mother or teacher help you to learn the important things about running your machine.

They all use two threads: a spool on top and a smaller spool underneath, called a bobbin. Each part must be threaded exactly right, or the machine will not stitch correctly. Even one little mistake will make everything come out wrong, so be sure you understand how to thread your machine before you start.

The machine is run by either a foot pedal or a knee lever. Practice running these controls with no thread in the machine, until you learn to make it go as fast or slow as you wish.

A good way to learn to stitch in a straight line is to stitch over lined paper, with no thread. The needle will punch holes in the paper.

When you are ready to start practicing on cloth, a seam guide will be helpful. Some machines have a special metal attachment for this, or you can buy a magnetic one to fit any machine. If you do not have either of these, a strip of cardboard taped on next to the presser foot will do very well (Fig. 12).

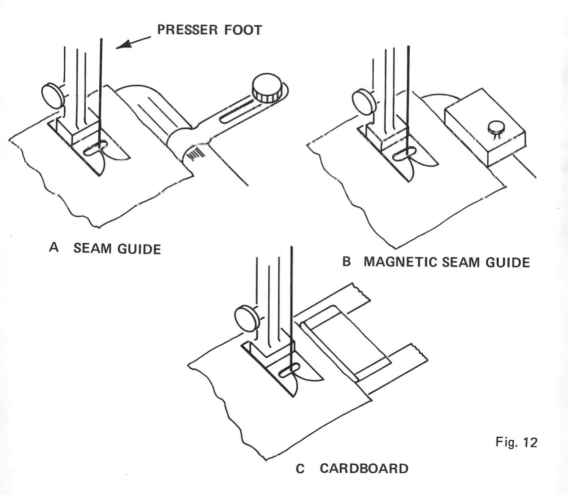

PRESSER FOOT

A SEAM GUIDE

B MAGNETIC SEAM GUIDE

C CARDBOARD

Fig. 12

As you stitch, hold the edge of your material right against the metal guide or cardboard, and watch the guide, rather than the presser foot, as you stitch.

Learn to use the backstitch lever, if your machine has this. At the beginning and end of your seam, stitch backward for three or four stitches, to prevent the seam from pulling out.

The newest machines can be set to make a zigzag stitch (Fig. 13), and many can also make a number of fancy embroidery stitches. These are not at all hard to do, once the machine has been properly set for the pattern.

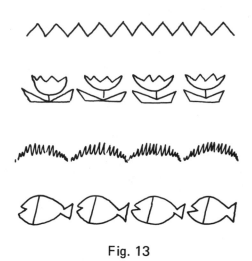

Fig. 13

CHAPTER TWO

MAKING FRINGE

FRINGING is not really sewing at all. It simply consists of pulling out threads along the edge of a piece of fabric. It makes a very pretty decorative edge by itself, or can be combined with other sewing methods, such as embroidery, or appliqué (which means sewing on small pieces of different fabrics to make a design).

Materials best suited for fringing have a plain, rather loose weave. Linen is good, and so-called rayon butcher linen works well and costs much less. You can also use plain or printed cottons, and plaid or checked is especially attractive. Burlap fringes very nicely, but is not suitable for something that needs to be washed often.

The important thing with fringing is to cut your material with a perfectly straight edge. You can do this by pulling one thread across your material, then cutting across the line where the thread was pulled out (Fig. 14).

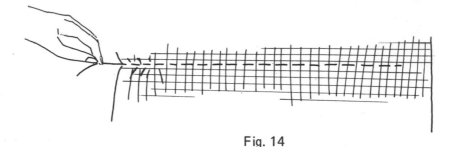

Fig. 14

If your material is very loose-woven, start by making a line of machine stitching at the distance from the edge where you want your fringe to end (Fig. 15). Then pull one thread at a time, picking it out with a pin at one end and pulling straight across. If you work right over a waste-basket, it will save you a lot of cleaning up later!

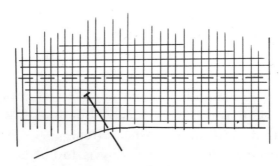

Fig. 15

A set of *place mats* with matching napkins makes a very attractive and useful gift. A good size for the mats is about 15 by 18 or 20 inches. As most material is 45 inches wide, you can get three 15-inch-wide mats out of one width, then cut them as long as you like in the other direction.

First, trim off about ¼ inch from the selvages of the fabric. The selvage is the firmly woven finished edge that runs along both long sides of a bolt of cloth.

Straighten the end, divide the width of the fabric into three equal parts by pulling threads, and cut along the lines. Pull a crosswise thread at the length you decide on, and cut across at that point (Fig. 16). Cut as many mats as you need.

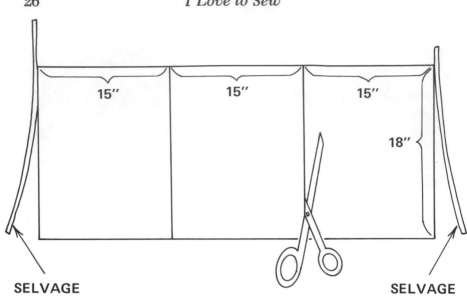

SELVAGE   SELVAGE

Fig. 16

If you want to make fringe all the way around, make a line of machine stitching on all four sides, about ¾ inch or 1 inch from the edge. Use the seam guide on the machine to keep it even (Fig. 17).

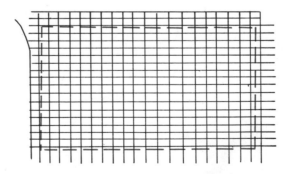

Fig. 17

You might like to fringe just the two short ends, and make a hem on the two long ends. Follow the directions for hemming in Chapter One, or use a strip of iron-on material (Stitch Witchery or Wonder Under), and press under the hem (Fig. 18).

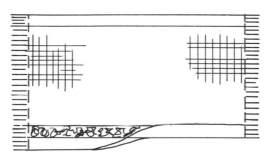

Fig. 18

Make a set of napkins to match. You can get four 11-inch-square napkins out of one width of material.

The mats and napkins can be left plain, or if you have a machine that will do embroidery, you can make a decorative border, either along the two short ends, as in the photograph, or around all four sides. Using a ruler, draw a *light* chalk line as a guide for the rows.

You could also *iron on a design,* using Wonder Under. This is a sticky material with a paper backing, and can be bought in most fabric shops. Complete directions are printed on it.

Use a lightweight cotton, slightly larger than your finished design, and press a piece of Wonder Under onto the back of it. Use as many different colors as you need for your design, and draw each part of the design on the paper backing. Be sure it is facing the *opposite* direction to the finished design, as you are working on the *wrong* side (Fig. 19).

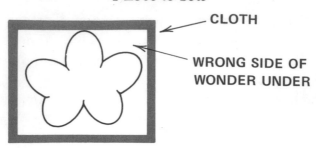

Fig. 19

Cut out the design, and carefully peel off the paper. Put your cutout pieces into position on the place mat, with the sticky side down, and press over it with a steam iron for ten seconds. When it cools, it will stay firmly in place. (Warning: Occasionally you will find materials that do not

stick well, so test a scrap of your fabric before going ahead with the finished work.)

A square of 45-inch material, fringed on all four sides, will make a cover for a bridge table. You can use a longer piece of 45-inch material to make a cloth for an oblong table. A bold plaid in gingham or linen would be attractive for this.

You may have ideas of your own for different sizes of fringed cloths. For instance, try a long narrow table runner, fringed on the short ends, hemmed on the sides, with designs ironed on if you like.

The skirt described in Chapter Six could be made with fringe at the bottom instead of a hem (Fig. 20).

Fig. 20

A *scarf* or sash can be made of a soft silky material or lightweight cotton. Measure a piece of fabric of the length you want the finished scarf to be, and twice as wide. Mark the width of the fringe with a row of stitching across both short ends. Fold it in half lengthwise, with the right side on the inside. Pin the edges together and stitch in a narrow seam, starting and stopping at the points where the fringe will begin (Fig. 21).

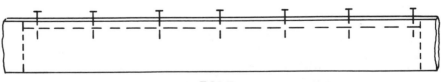

FOLD

Fig. 21

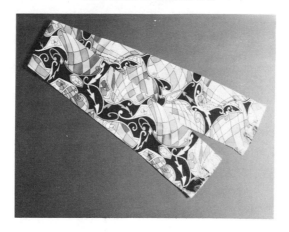

Turn the scarf right side out, press the seam flat, and fringe the ends.

Fringe can also be used to finish the wall hangings in Chapter Four.

Place mats, napkins, or table covers can be decorated with hand embroidery.

You will need cotton embroidery floss, which comes with six strands twisted together. You can pull it apart and use as many strands as you like.

Use a needle with a large, long eye, and an embroidery hoop is a good idea if you are going to work on a fairly large area, as it will keep the fabric from pulling out of shape. Place the smaller hoop under the cloth, then put the larger one over it and press down (Fig. 22).

Fig. 22

The *outline* stitch can be used to outline a complete design, or to pick out details, as in the appliqué butterfly on the checked place mat.

Mark a straight line with chalk on your cloth. Work from left to right, and start by knotting your thread and bringing it up from underneath.

Put your needle in at the length of stitch you want (about ½ inch for coarse work), and bring it out again to the left, half way back to where the thread came out (Fig. 16).

Put the needle in again ½ inch forward and back up through the same hole as the end of the last stitch (Fig. 23). Keep the thread pushed up away from your work.

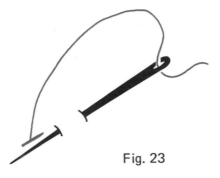

Fig. 23

Continue making a row of stitches, always bringing the needle back up at the end of the last stitch. Your stitches as they overlap will make a very solid line (Fig. 24).

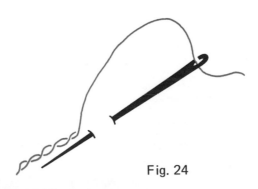

Fig. 24

When you are making a curved line, keep turning your work so you are always sewing in the same direction.

With most embroidery stitches, finish it off on the back by weaving the needle back through the under side of the stitches (Fig. 25), and cut the thread off close.

Try using your own ideas to work out needlework designs. Start with a drawing you made in art class, or find ideas in picture books or printed fabrics.

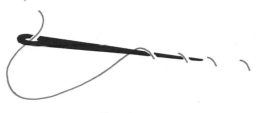

Fig. 25

Lazy daisy stitch, used for making flowers or leaves.

Mark a light circle as a guide, and bring up the thread in the center. Put the needle in next to where the end came out, and bring it out against the edge of the circle (Fig. 26), with the thread pulled under the needle point. Pull it through until the thread lies flat. Put the needle down on the opposite side of the loop you made, and bring it up in the center again (Fig. 27). Repeat around the circle until it is filled (Fig. 28).

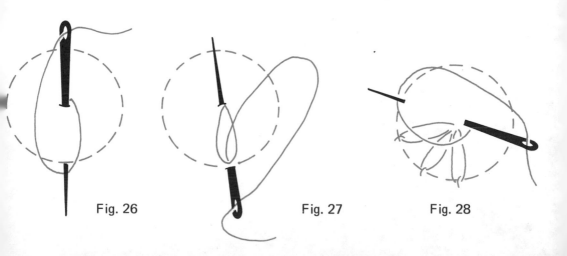

Fig. 26   Fig. 27   Fig. 28

French knots can be used to make the center of a flower—use one or several knots—or anywhere that you want a small circle to mark a detail.

Bring the thread up from underneath, make a small stitch next to it, leaving the needle with about ½ inch coming out. Wind the thread twice around the needle (Fig. 29), and pull it through, holding the knot with your thumbnail to keep it from tangling (Fig. 30).

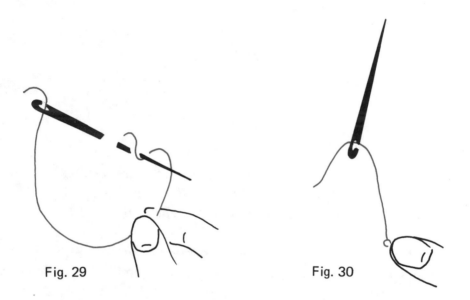

Fig. 29   Fig. 30

Put the needle in again close to the knot (Fig. 31). You can use more threads in your needle for a heavier knot.

Fig. 31

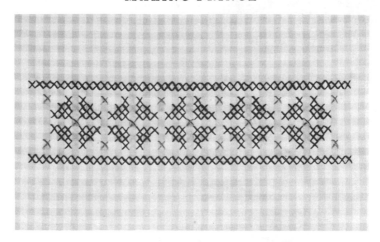

The *cross-stitch* makes a pretty border design for checked gingham place mats or a table cloth. It is easy to follow the checks to keep your stitches straight and exactly the same size.

The design shown in this photo is made with ¼-inch checked material, with 3 strands of embroidery cotton.

The solid rows are worked by making one slanting stitch in each square until you reach the end of the row. Put your needle in at the top corner of a square and bring it out at the corner directly below (Fig. 32).

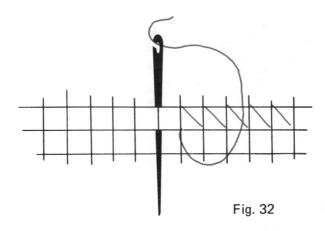

Fig. 32

At the end of the row, change directions and fill in with stitches slanting in the opposite direction (Fig. 33).

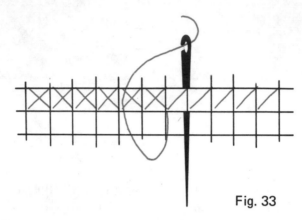

Fig. 33

When making stitches in a more scattered design, you can complete each cross before going on to the next.

To finish off the thread on the back, put your needle under a thread and make a knot around it, as in making a French knot (Fig. 34).

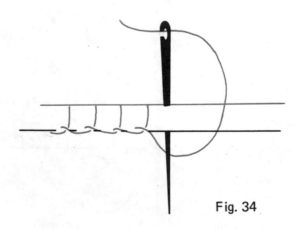

Fig. 34

CHAPTER THREE

ACCESSORIES

A GOOD WAY to use leftover pieces of material from sewing projects is to make matching accessories. For instance, there may be enough leftover fabric from a big project like a dress to make a matching tote bag, scarf, or hat.

Of course, any of these same things can be made of other materials, to contrast with your outfit.

Unlined drawstring bag. This can be any size—a small or medium-size handbag, or a large tote bag for carrying sewing or knitting, extra shoes, school books, etc.

This one shown here started with a piece of cotton material 16½ by 36 inches. It was cut so that the squares in the design would come out even on both sides.

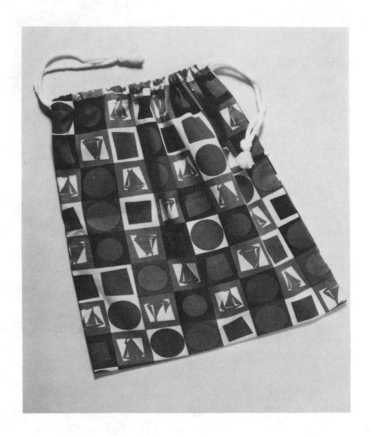

Fold the material in half, right sides together, across the short way. The fold makes the bottom of the bag (Fig. 35).

Pin and stitch both long edges in a ½-inch seam, ending the stitching 3 inches from the top.

Hem the four short edges at the top by pressing under ½ inch, and stitch close to the edge (Fig. 36).

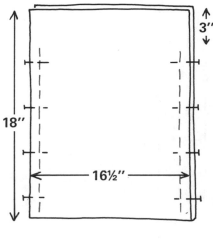

Fig. 35

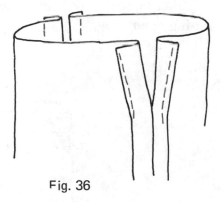

Fig. 36

To make a casing at the top, press under ¼ inch on both top edges, then turn under 1 inch and pin in place every few inches (Fig. 37).

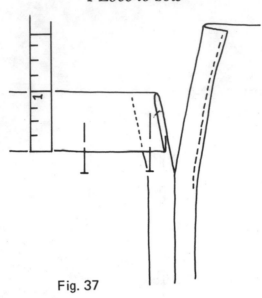

Fig. 37

Stitch close to the pinned edge, leaving the ends of the casing open (Fig. 38).

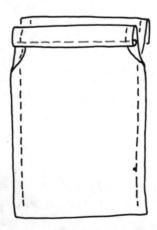

Fig. 38

Turn the bag right side out. For drawstrings, cut two pieces of white cable cord about 2½ times the width of the bag. Pull one cord through the opening by attaching a safety pin to one end (Fig. 39). (The cord should first be wrapped with Scotch tape to prevent raveling.) Bring the cord out one end, then back through the casing on the other side, and knot the ends together.

Take the second piece of cord and pull it through the casing the same way, but starting at the opposite side (Fig. 40). Knot the ends.

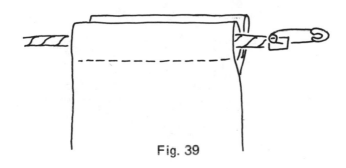

Fig. 39

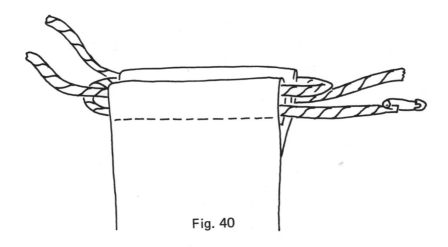

Fig. 40

This *bag* is trimmed with fancy woven braid; 3 yards are needed for this size. You will need a piece of firm cotton or linen in a plain color, 12 by 26 inches, and a piece of figured or contrasting material of the same size for the lining.

Place one of your rectangles of fabric on top of the other, with right sides together, pin around the edges, and stitch in a ½-inch seam, leaving about 4 inches open on one long edge, through which to turn the bag right side out (Fig. 41). Trim off all four corners as shown.

Turn right side out, pull the seam edges out, using a pin or needle to get a good square corner (Fig. 42).

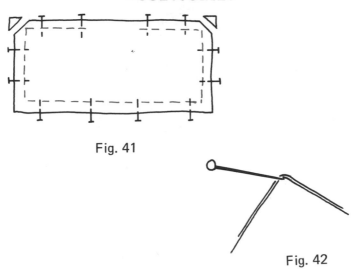

Fig. 41

Fig. 42

Press the edges flat, folding under the opening at the side.

The braid forms trimming and handles all in one. On the right side, mark a light chalk line 2½ inches from both long edges. Starting in the middle of one long side, pin the braid along the chalk line (Fig. 43). Allow 12 inches for the handle, fold the braid around and start pinning 2½ inches from the other side, continue to the other end, make another handle 12 inches long, and pin the rest of the tape until it meets the end where you started.

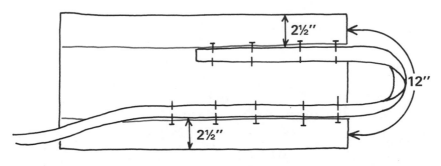

Fig. 43

Turn under the end of the braid and let it overlap about ½ inch (Fig. 44).

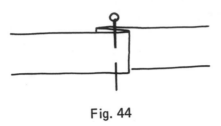

Fig. 44

Stitch close to both edges of the braid, backstitch at both ends, and leave the handles free (Fig. 45).

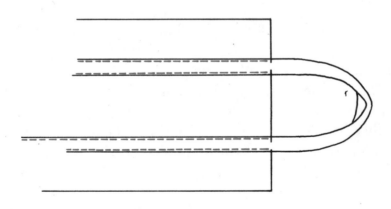

Fig. 45

To make stronger handles, pin another strip of tape to the back of each handle, with the wrong sides together. (Or use plain grosgrain ribbon of the same width.) Stitch close to both edges (Fig. 46).

Fold the bag in half crosswise, pin along both sides, and stitch ¼ inch from the edges (Fig. 47).

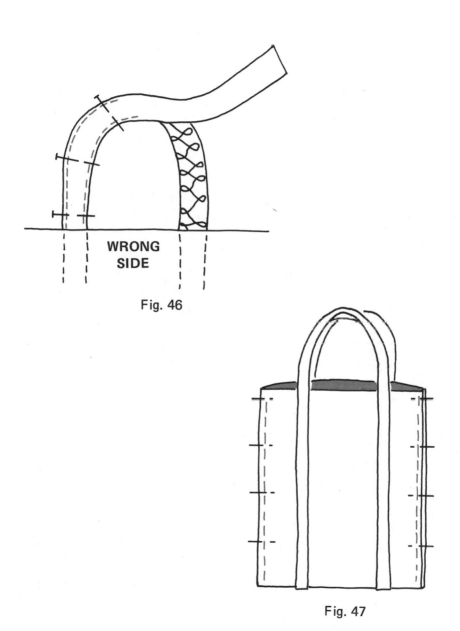

WRONG
SIDE

Fig. 46

Fig. 47

A *small envelope bag* to use for dressy occasions. This one was made of lightweight wool, with yarn trim, and a cotton print lining. It could be made to match or contrast with your winter coat.

Besides the outside material and lining, you will need a stiff interfacing. Ask for buckram or crinoline at the fabric store.

Use this diagram (Fig. 48) to cut each of the three parts: outside, lining, and interfacing.

Pin the interfacing to the wrong side of the wool fabric, and machine baste ⅜ inch from the edges. Trim off the extra interfacing close to the stitching (Fig. 49).

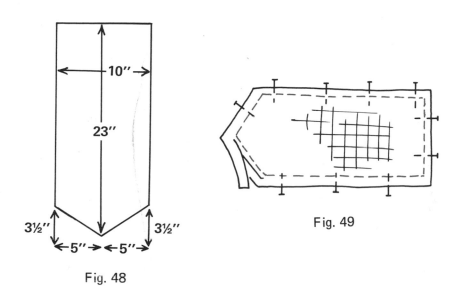

Fig. 48

Fig. 49

Place the wool and the lining fabrics with right sides together, pin and stitch ½ inch from edges, leaving a 4-inch opening on one long edge. Trim off the corners (Fig. 50).

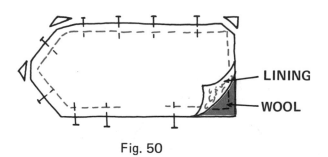

LINING

WOOL

Fig. 50

Turn and press it the same as for the previous tote bag.

Fold up the bottom 7½ inches, pin and stitch both sides ¼ inch from the edges (Fig. 51).

Fold down the front flap and fasten the point with a snap (Fig. 52).

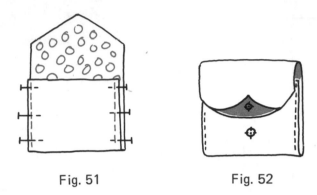

Fig. 51   Fig. 52

The handle is made of six strands of heavy rug yarn braided together. Cut the yarn a few inches longer than you want the finished handle. Tie a piece of yarn tightly around all the strands near the end, pin it to something solid, and braid, using two strands together (Fig. 53).

Fig. 53

Sew each end to the back of the bag, going over all strands several times. Leave 2 inches for fringe, and trim evenly (Fig. 54).

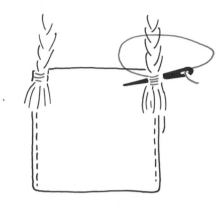

Fig. 54

Make a tassel for the front by wrapping yarn around a piece of heavy paper 3 inches wide. Slip a piece of yarn under all layers, and tie tightly (Fig. 55).

Pull out the paper, wrap one end of the piece of yarn several times around one end of the bunch of strands, and tie tightly (Fig. 56). Trim evenly across the looped ends, and sew the knotted end to the point of the bag (Fig. 57).

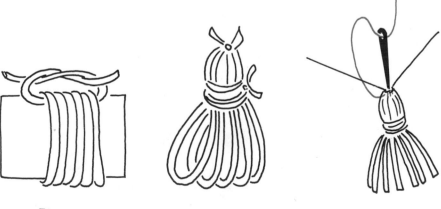

Fig. 55   Fig. 56   Fig. 57

Belts are easy to make, and can be any length or width you like. It can be a long tie sash, or a short belt with a buckle.

Take a straight piece of cotton print fabric, as long as the finished belt and twice as wide, plus 1 inch for the seam.

Fold it in half the long way, right sides together, pin, and stitch in a ½-inch seam on the long edge and across both ends. The ends can be cut on a slant if you like. Leave an opening in the center of the long edge (Fig. 58).

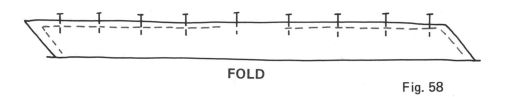

FOLD

Fig. 58

Trim the corners and turn right side out by folding each end over a pencil or ruler, and rolling it back (Fig. 59).

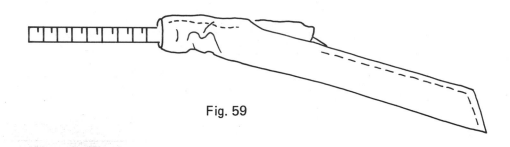

Fig. 59

Press the edges flat and sew the opening together with small overcasting stitches (Fig. 60).

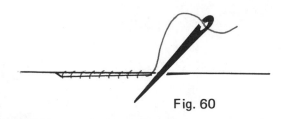

Fig. 60

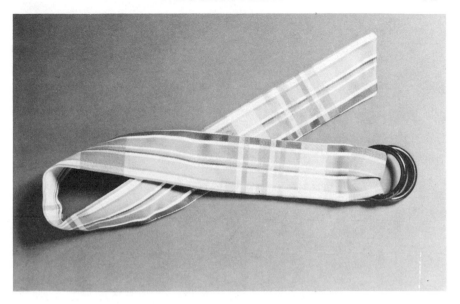

Buckled belt. Make it the correct waist measurement plus 8 inches. One short end should be straight.

You can buy sets of two rings for a buckle. Fold the straight end through both rings and hand sew on the back (Fig. 61).

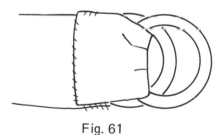

Fig. 61

Fasten by pulling the other end of the belt through the two rings from underneath, then back through the lower ring.

Three-cornered head scarves can be made in various sizes. This small one is double, and can be worn on either the figured or plain side. Start with a square corner of your fabric (line it up on the corner of a table to be sure it is square) (Fig. 62). Measure 14 inches along both sides, and connect the two points, using a yardstick and chalk. Cut a second triangle of the lining fabric.

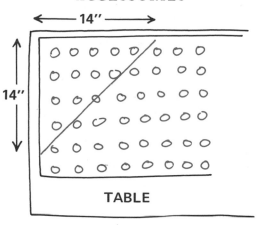

Fig. 62

Cut two ties, 13 inches long, of narrow ribbon or double-fold bias binding. (If using binding, stitch along the open edge.)

Place the two triangles with right sides together, and put the ties inside the two sharp corners, matching one end with the point, and with the rest of the tie inside (Fig. 63). (Be sure the ties are pulled in toward the center, so they will not get stitched into the seams.)

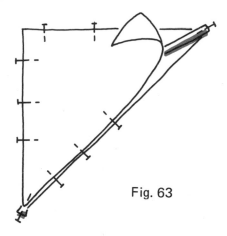

Fig. 63

Pin, and stitch in a ⅜-inch seam, leaving an opening in one side, and make three stitches across the tie in each corner (Fig. 64). Stitch very slowly as you come to each corner. To turn the corners, leave the machine needle in the cloth, lift the presser foot, turn the material on the needle, then lower the presser foot.

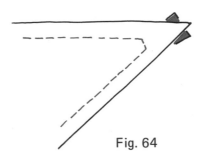

Fig. 64

Trim the corners, turn right side out, and sew the opening by hand.

Larger scarves can be made without the tie ends. A good size is 24 inches. For lightweight materials, make it double, or for heavier fabric use just one layer and make a narrow hem around the three sides. Press under ¼ inch, then turn in again ¼ inch, pin, and hem by hand or stitch close to the edge (Fig. 65).

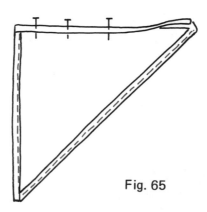

Fig. 65

Ruffled hat. Start with an 18-inch circle. (For a baby's hat, use a 16-inch circle.)

To make a circle pattern, put a pin through the end of a tape measure and down through the center of a piece of paper. Swing the tape in an arc, marking the correct length every few inches. (This length should be ½ the length of the finished circle.) You might have a large round tray or plate that can be traced.

Use a patterned fabric for one side and a plain color for the other, and it can be worn on either side. Place the two fabrics with right sides together, pin on the circle pattern, and cut both pieces together.

Remove the pattern, pin around the edges of the hat, and stitch in a ½-inch seam (Fig. 66), leaving a small opening. Turn right side out and press, and sew up the opening by hand.

To make a casing for the elastic, mark another circle 1¼ inches from the edge, by making a smaller circle pattern and drawing around it *lightly* with chalk. Put in a few pins to keep the two layers from slipping apart, and stitch on the chalk line (Fig. 67).

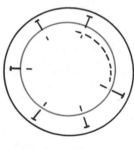

Fig. 66

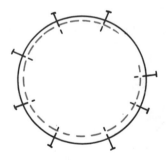

Fig. 67

Stitch a second row ½ inch inside the first row. You should be able to guide it evenly by watching the edge of the presser foot, keeping it just inside the first row.

Use ¼-inch-wide elastic to gather the edge of the hat. Measure around your head for a snug fit, with an extra inch to overlap. With pointed scissors, cut a small slit through one layer only of the casing (Fig. 68). Pin a small safety pin to one end of the elastic, and another one crosswise on the other end, and pull the elastic all the way through the casing, gathering the edge as you go.

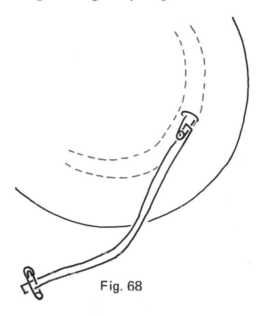

Fig. 68

Pull both ends out through the slit, overlap the ends 1 inch and pin (Fig. 69). Try it on and adjust to fit, then overcast both edges of the elastic very firmly (Fig. 70), and let it slip back inside the casing.

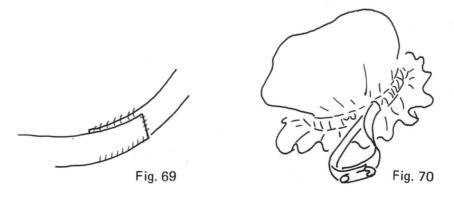

Fig. 69   Fig. 70

CHAPTER FOUR

DECORATIONS
AROUND THE HOUSE

BEDSPREAD, curtains, and pillows, in matching or contrasting material, will do a great deal to dress up a plain room.

Quite a few yards of material will be needed, so shop around for good buys in printed or plain cotton. It can be drapery fabric, or regular dress material will do, and is usually less expensive.

For *curtains,* use a full width of 36-inch- or 45-inch-wide fabric for each panel. Find the correct length by measuring your window, following the diagram in Fig. 71. For a full-length curtain, measure from the top of the frame to the

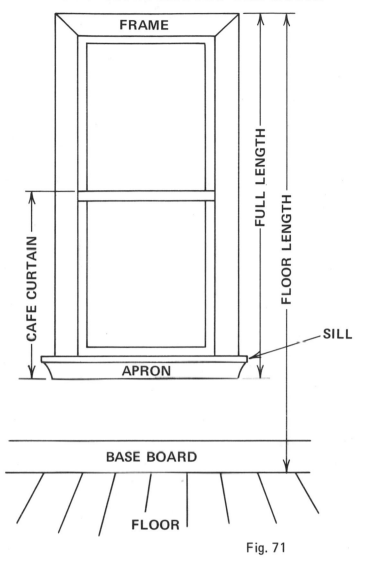

Fig. 71

bottom of the apron, and add 5 inches for hems. If you prefer floor-length curtains, measure down to the floor. For a café curtain, measure from the center crossbar of the window to the bottom of the apron.

Each window will need two full lengths, plus hems. Figure how much you will need for each window, and multiply by the number of windows before you buy your material.

Most lightweight curtain materials can be torn straight across, which simplifies your cutting job. Clip through the selvage (Fig. 72), then tear across until you reach the

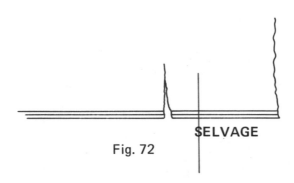

SELVAGE

Fig. 72

opposite selvage, which should be cut. Try this on a scrap first, and if the material does not tear easily, you will have to cut it. Measure the length along the selvages, and again along the lengthwise fold, mark with chalk, and connect the two marks, using a yardstick and chalk (Fig. 73). Cut along the line.

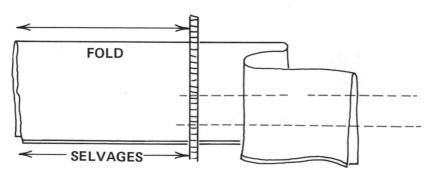

FOLD

SELVAGES

Fig. 73

If the selvages of the fabric look neat, you can just leave them as a finish for the sides of the curtains. Often there is printing along the selvage, or a different color, and in this case both selvages should be pressed under and stitched (Fig. 74).

Fig. 74

Divide the hem allowance evenly between top and bottom. On both ends, press under ½ inch, then turn up a 2-inch hem, measuring in several places, and pin along the edge (Fig. 75). Stitch close to the folded edge.

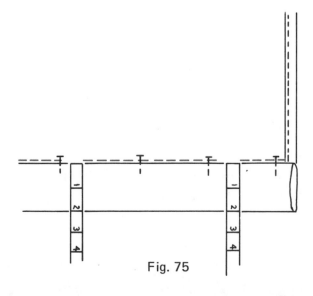

Fig. 75

At the top of the curtain, you will need to make another row of stitching, ¾ inch from the top (Fig. 76). This makes

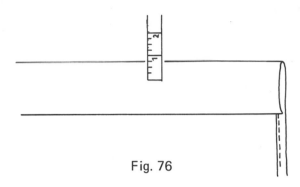

Fig. 76

what is called a heading. The curtain rod is slipped between the two rows of stitching, and the upper section forms a ruffle (Fig. 77).

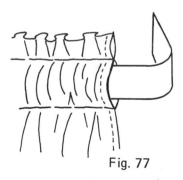

Fig. 77

If you make a short café curtain, you might make a ruffle or valance to cover the top of the window. Cut two pieces of fabric about 15 inches long, and sew the two short ends together in a narrow seam (Fig. 78). Press the seam open,

Fig. 78

then finish the hems the same as the other curtains. (Fig. 79 gives drawings of curtains.)

The long curtains may be tied back with fabric strips or cording, if you like.

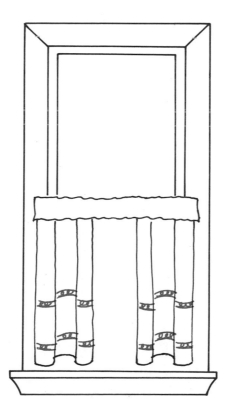

Fig. 79

A plain *bedspread* can be made of two lengths of material, with a seam running down the center. Measure the length needed to cover the top of your bed, with enough to hang down to the floor at the foot (Fig. 80). Add an extra 12 inches to tuck under the pillow. Cut two pieces in this length.

Stitch two of the long edges together in a narrow seam and press open.

Place the spread over the bed with the seam exactly in the center, to see how much hem needs to be taken up on the two long sides. Let it just clear the floor, then add one inch hem allowance on each side. Tear off the extra width (Fig. 81).

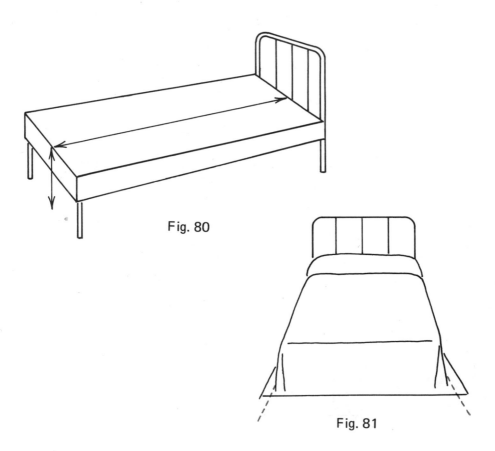

Fig. 80

Fig. 81

Press up ½ inch on all four sides, then turn up another ½ inch, pin, and stitch the hem.

If the material is a plain color, you can add fancy braid to cover the seam, then add several more rows of braid to form a design. Be sure to measure carefully so the braid is an even distance from the edges (Fig. 82). Have more rows of braid crossing over in the opposite direction if you wish. The curtains could also be trimmed with the same braid.

It would be fun to design a bedspread with a large, bold appliqué design.

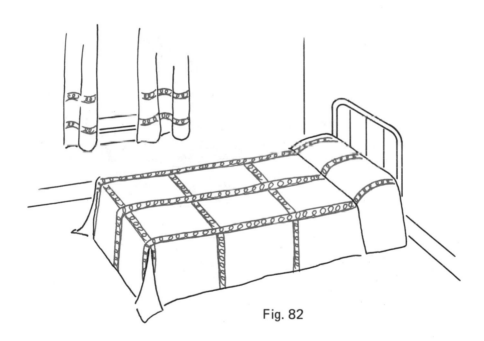

Fig. 82

Fig. 83 shows a design with assorted squares, triangles, and circles cut out of bright colors. Fig. 84 has giant-size flowers peeking over a fence made of striped fabric.

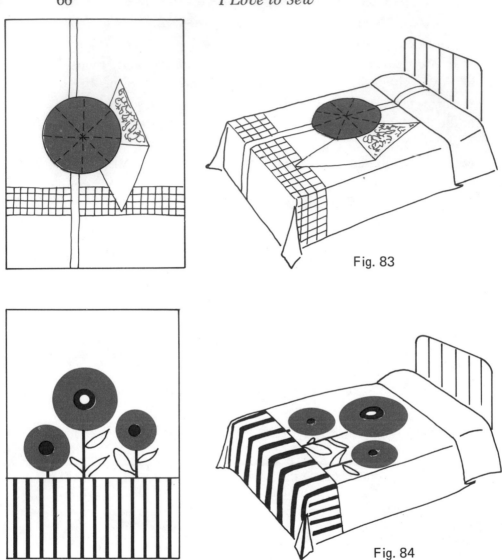

Fig. 83

Fig. 84

Cut out each section of the design, press under ¼ inch on all sides, arrange them on the background, and pin in place. (It might be best to do this with everything spread out on the floor.) Stitch close to the edges of each piece, with either plain or zigzag stitch (Fig. 85).

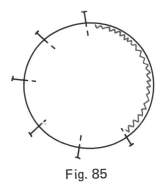

Fig. 85

Decorative pillows help to make a room seem cozy and comfortable. Make some for your own room, or for gifts. The size and shape can be whatever you like, but the method is the same. Cut two squares or oblongs of the same size. The material could match something else in the room, or

small remnants of upholstery fabric can be used. Designs can be added in appliqué or embroidery—see Chapter Two. The design should be finished before the pillow is put together.

You will need an inner pillow, as well as the outside cover, to hold the stuffing, so that the cover can be taken off and washed or cleaned when necessary. Use any plain material (discarded sheets will do very well), cut two pieces the same size as the pillow, pin the two pieces together and stitch in a ½-inch seam, leaving an opening of 4 to 5 inches (Fig. 86). Turn right side out and put in

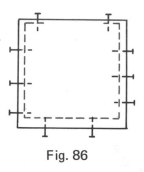

Fig. 86

the stuffing through the opening until the pillow is nice and plump. Polyester fiber can be bought in large bags, and makes a nice soft filling, or if someone in your family has a lot of old nylon panty hose or stockings with runs (these are usually very plentiful!) they can be cut up fine and used for filling.

When the pillow is full, turn in the rest of the seam and overcast the edges together (Fig. 87).

The outside pillow is made the same way. Place the right sides together, pin and stitch, leaving most of one end open. Stitch just around the corners (Fig. 88).

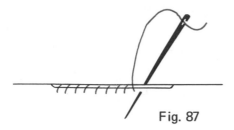

Fig. 87

Fig. 88

If you want to put fringe around the pillow, this must be sewn between the two layers of fabric. Pin the fringe around the four sides of one piece, with the edges of the fringe facing in, and the woven edge against the edge of the fabric. Make a small pleat in the fringe at each corner. Baste in place (Fig. 89).

Fig. 89

Stitch the fringe along the end that will be left open.
Put the other half of the pillow face down over the fringe,
pin, and stitch the other three sides (Fig. 90).

When the pillow is turned right side out, the fringe will
face outward. Put the inner pillow inside the cover, pulling
it carefully into all the corners.

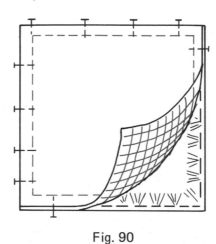

Fig. 90

Turn in the seam allowance against the fringe, pin, and
slipstitch against the fringed edge (Fig. 91).

Pillows do not have to be square. They can be round,
triangular, or in any fancy shape.

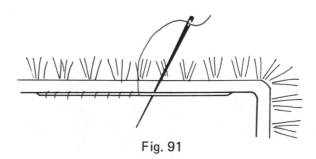

Fig. 91

Simple *fruit* or *vegetable shapes* cut out of felt are fun. Make a giant-size carrot, pea pod, pear, apple, pineapple, strawberry, etc. (Fig. 92).

First draw and cut a paper pattern, using some of the sketches in Fig. 92, or design your own. Pin the pattern on a double thickness of felt and cut out. Use the same pattern to make an inner pillow of cotton fabric.

Make a separate pattern for the leaves and cut out of a double piece of green felt.

Mark the details on the fruit with embroidery (refer to Chapter Two), pieces of felt cut to shape and sewn on, rickrack, or strips of tape or ribbon. Then pin the two main pieces together and stitch in a very narrow seam on the *right* side. Leave an opening big enough to insert the inner pillow.

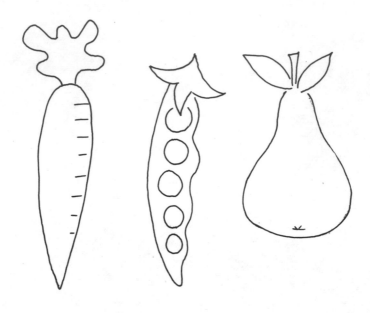

Fig. 92

When making leaves, put a small amount of stuffing between the two layers, then stitch all around the edges. This
gives the leaves more body and stiffness.

Before stitching the seam on the fruit, insert the base of
the leaves between the two layers of fruit, pin, and stitch
all layers together (Fig. 93).

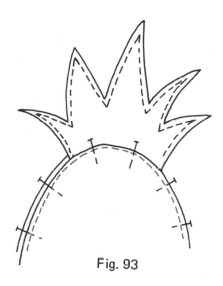

Fig. 93

Put the inner pillow inside and pin and stitch the opening. A zipper foot on the sewing machine will make this job
easier.

The strawberry in the photo has a sprinkling of seeds done
with black yarn in a running stitch, with small stitches on
top and longer stitches on the wrong side. The leaves are
made separately and sewn in place with a few hand stitches
at the point where the three leaves meet. The blossom is
sewn just through the center, so the petals are loose.

You can help to make your closet look neat and pretty by making *matching covers* for a collection of old wire coat hangers, or make a set of these for a gift.

Use felt or any pretty woven fabric. Start with a double layer of fabric, right sides together, place a coat hanger over this and trace around it with chalk (Fig. 94). Let the lower edge extend about 2 inches below the hanger. Pin along the chalk line and cut out, leaving ½ inch beyond the line for a seam allowance.

Stitch along the seam line, leaving 1 inch open at the top center, and leave the lower edge open also (Fig. 95).

Turn right side out, turn in the top opening, and turn up and finish a hem at the bottom. You may stitch lace, rickrack, or braid over the edge. Slip the cover over the hanger and tie a ribbon bow at the top (Fig. 96). Embroidered or appliqué trim can be used. (Refer to Chapter Two.) This should be done before the two sections are stitched together.

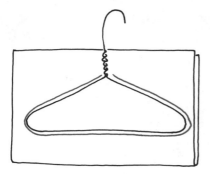

Fig. 94

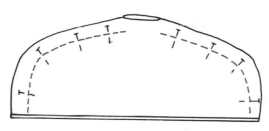

Fig. 95

Fig. 96

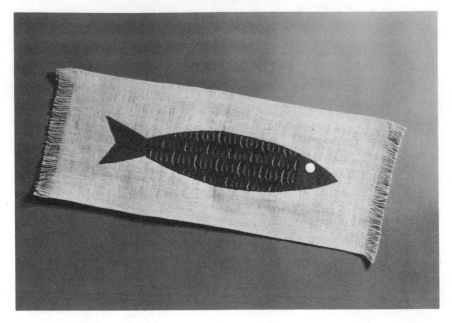

This fish design for a *wall hanging* is made of turquoise burlap, with the fish's body cut out of a fancy blue, green, and black wool, with deep blue felt for the head and tail. The body is ironed in place with Wonder Under, then the edge is outlined in black by machine with a very close zig-zag stitch. The head and tail are sewn by hand, and the eye is a white button. The short ends are fringed, and the top and bottom hems ironed down.

A large and more elaborate hanging is fun to make if you want to spend time on a long project. You can base it on one of your own drawings, or perhaps a page from a favorite picture book. Another way is to cut shapes out of different-colored fabrics and move them around on the background until a design is suggested. Make your design by stitching or hand sewing the pieces (woven fabrics must have ¼ inch pressed under the edges first, or they will fray). The larger areas could also be ironed in place. Finally, add the finishing details with embroidery (see Chapter Two).

A large hanging should be hung on a wooden dowel.

When cutting the background fabric, leave an extra 2 inches on all sides. Mark the outside edge of your design with chalk, and press under the two sides and bottom edge along the line (Fig. 97).

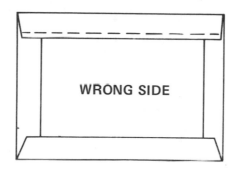

WRONG SIDE

Fig. 97

When finished, the back should be covered with a piece of plain cotton to cover the back of the stitches, and also to add extra body and stiffness to the hanging.

Cut the backing the same size as the finished hanging, then press under ½ inch on three sides, 1 inch at the top. Center it evenly on the back of the hanging, pin, and slipstitch to the edges by hand, taking care not to sew through to the front (Fig. 98).

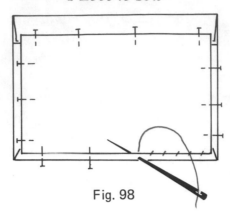

Fig. 98

Put a dowel through the hem and hang with a cord (Fig. 99).

Fig. 99

CHAPTER FIVE

TOYS

STUFFED TOYS are fun to make. Many girls like to use them to decorate their rooms, or they are ideal gifts for younger children.

They can be made of felt, using the method described for the fruit and vegetable-shaped pillows in Chapter Four, but in this chapter you will learn how to make them of cotton or wool fabrics.

You can design your own animals if you choose a simple shape that does not have projecting legs or arms. Each animal should be made like a pillow, with identical pieces for front and back. Sometimes ears, tails, etc. can be stitched between the two layers. Picture books will suggest ideas, or use some of the following designs.

The *fish* can be short and fat, or a long, thin oval. The tail is in one piece with the fish, and the fins are cut separately.

Draw the design on fairly heavy paper, and cut it out. Use two thicknesses of your chosen material, with the right sides placed together, pin on the pattern, and trace around it with a pencil or chalk (Fig. 100). This line will be the

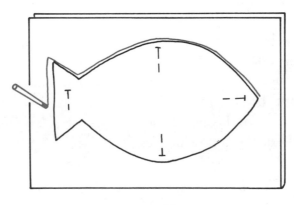

Fig. 100

stitching line. Make another line ⅜ of an inch outside the first line as a seam allowance. Cut along the second line (Fig. 101). Remove the pattern.

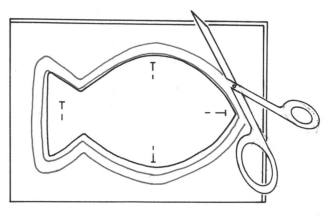

Fig. 101

The fins can be cut of felt, in triangles or four-sided pieces. Cut two small fins for the lower front, two larger ones for the sides, and a triangle and a four-sided piece for the back fins (Fig. 102).

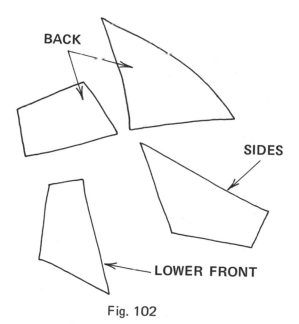

BACK

SIDES

LOWER FRONT

Fig. 102

On the right side of one piece of the fish's body, place the two upper back fins at the top and the two small fins at the bottom, turned toward the inside, and pin (Fig. 103).

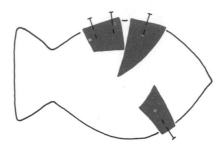

Fig. 103

The fins will be enclosed in the seam, and will be on the outside when the fish is turned right side out.

Place the other half of the fish, with the stitching line, on top of the first half, pin the edges, and stitch along the pencil line, leaving about 3 to 4 inches open for turning (Fig. 104).

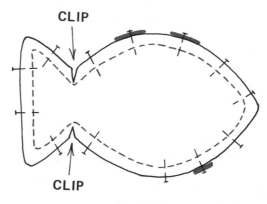

Fig. 104

Before turning, be sure to clip all inside corners almost up to the stitching (Fig. 104).

Turn right side out and stuff. (Polyester fiber or old cup-up nylons are good to use.) Turn in the open edges, pin, and overcast by hand (Fig. 105).

Sew the other two fins to the sides, sewing just across one end. Sew a button on each side for the eyes, and make a mouth with outline stitch in black.

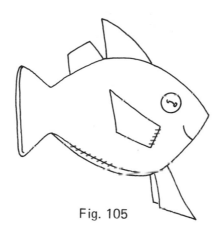

Fig. 105

A *turtle* is made with a circle for a body. (Trace a plate of the size you prefer.) Cut the feet, tail, and head of felt, using patterns in Fig. 106. Cut four feet, one tail, and two

Fig. 106

pieces for the head. First stitch the two pieces for the head close to the edges, leaving the end open, and stuff it (Fig. 107).

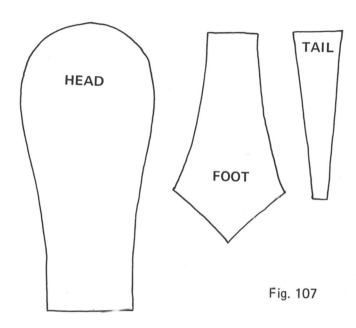

Fig. 107

Place the head, feet, and tail on one circle of cloth, as in Fig. 108, pin, and pin the other circle on top. Stitch and turn.

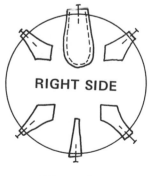

Fig. 108

Wide rickrack may be stitched around the outside edge of the turtle, before stuffing (Fig. 109). Be careful to leave the opening free, stitching only over the top layer. Then stuff, sew up the opening, and sew two small buttons on the head for eyes.

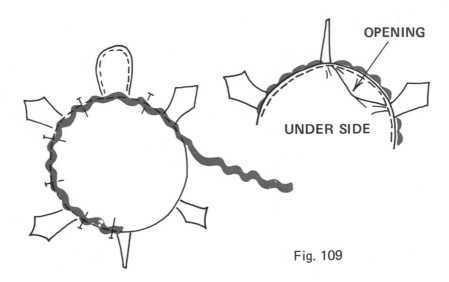

Fig. 109

Children seem to enjoy creepy crawly pets. Here is a *friendly worm* for you to make. Use two long narrow strips of fabric any size you like. (This one is 5 inches by 23 inches.) Round off both ends.

Legs are made of two strips of cotton fringe. Pin the fringe along the two long sides of one half of the worm, on the right side (Fig. 110). Pin the other half of the worm face down over it. Stitch ½ inch from the edges, leaving one end open. Turn, stuff, and sew up.

The eyes are made of a large flat button with a small round button sewn through the middle.

Tie pieces of bright yarn around the body, 2 to 3 inches apart. Antennae may be made of a pipe cleaner, bent to shape and sewn through the middle.

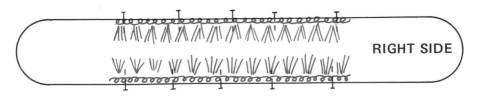

RIGHT SIDE

Fig. 110

The *cat* pattern is made of a large and a small circle. Trace two dishes of the size you want, letting them overlap, as in Fig. 111. Make a curved line at either side of the neck where the circles join.

Cut the cat out of two pieces of fabric, tracing around the pattern and adding a seam allowance. On the right side of one piece, draw lines for the tail and legs, and embroider with outline stitch in black (Fig. 112). (See embroidery stitches in Chapter Two.) Sew on felt circles for eyes, with a button in the middle, a pink triangle for a nose, and embroider the mouth and whiskers.

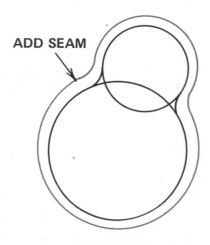

Fig. 111

Fig. 112

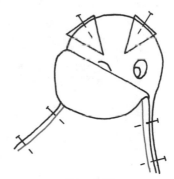

Fig. 113

Cut two triangles of felt for ears, pin as in Fig. 113, and pin on the second layer of fabric. Stitch, clip, turn, and finish as with the other animals. Put lace or ribbon around the neck.

Hand puppets can be made of felt. Work out one basic pattern, then add details of face, hair, and costume to make different characters. Try putting on a show by making characters from a favorite story, or make up your own comedy or musical skit. Several children can stand behind a screen or curtain, with just the hands showing (Fig. 114). Talk or sing for the puppets, or have them sing along with records.

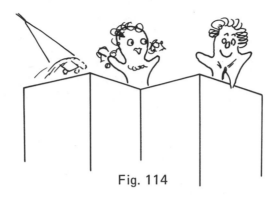

Fig. 114

Make a pattern by tracing a circle for the head—about
3½ to 4½ inches is a good size. Then place your hand on
the paper, and draw around it to make the body and arms
to fit over your hand, allowing plenty of room for motion
(Fig. 115). Make it long enough to come down over the
wrist.

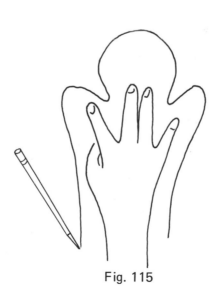

Fig. 115

Pin the pattern on a double piece of felt and cut out.

Cut pieces of felt, fabric, trimming, buttons, etc., and sew the face and costume details on the front half. Then stitch the two pieces together close to the edges, leaving the bottom open (Fig. 116). Stuff the head lightly with cotton. Hair, hats, and other accessories can be added last.

Fig. 117 shows several ideas for different characters. If desired, legs can be added to the front half only.

Fig. 116

BACK VIEW

Fig. 117

This *stuffed cube* is an ideal toy for a small baby. The one in the photo is made of six-inch squares. You could make a set of several small ones.

Cut six squares all the same size, each one of a different material. Use fabrics with interesting pictures or designs, or make letters or pictures of felt, and sew or iron them in place.

First sew four squares together in a strip, right sides together, in ¼-inch seams (Fig. 118). Then sew squares number 5 and 6 on either side of square number 2, ending the stitching ¼ inch from the ends of the squares (detail, Fig. 119).

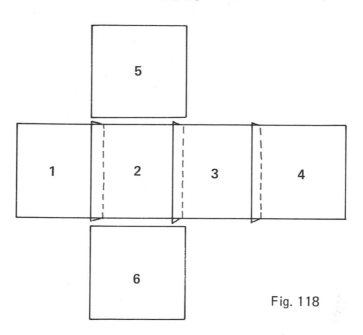

Fig. 118

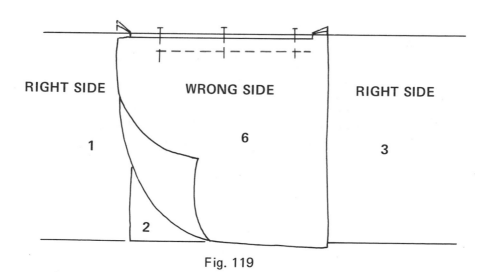

Fig. 119

Sew squares 1 and 4 together (Fig. 120).

Fold down squares 5 and 6, pin and stitch to the sides of squares 1, 3, and 4, having stitching end ¼ inch from each corner. Leave one seam open (Fig. 121). Turn, pin seams flat, and top stitch (Fig. 122).

Stuff the cube, sew up, and top stitch the remaining seam.

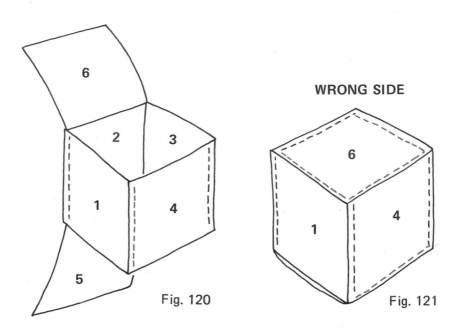

Fig. 120

WRONG SIDE

Fig. 121

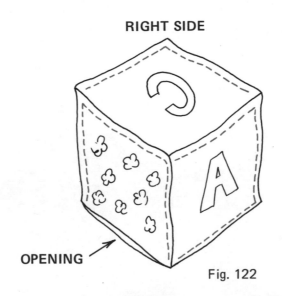

RIGHT SIDE

OPENING

Fig. 122

CHAPTER SIX

SIMPLE CLOTHING

THERE ARE SEVERAL simple articles of clothing that you can make without a pattern.

First is a *gathered skirt* with an elastic waist. For the short version, use one piece of material 45 inches wide, and find the length by measuring from your waist down to where you want the skirt to end. Add 4 inches for the hem and top heading.

Fold the fabric in half lengthwise, with right sides together, and pin and stitch the edges in a ½-inch seam, which will go in the center back (Fig. 123).

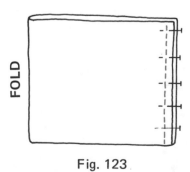

Fig. 123

Presss under ¼ inch on both top and bottom edges of the skirt. Turn down the top a second time, making a heading ¼ inch wider than the elastic, which should be ¾ inch or 1 inch wide. Check the width in several places with a ruler, and pin along the lower folded edge (Fig. 124).

Stitch close to both folded edges, leaving an opening in the lower edge at the seam, where the elastic will be put in (Fig. 125).

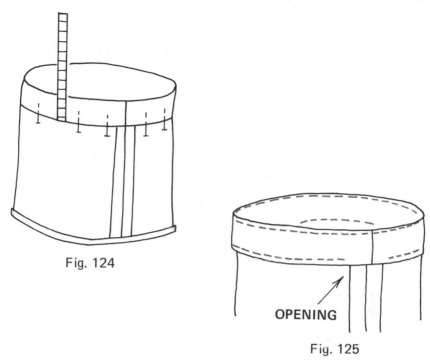

Fig. 124

OPENING

Fig. 125

Cut a piece of elastic just long enough to fit around your waist. Fasten a large safety pin to each end, put the first pin through the opening, and pull the elastic through, bringing it out again through the same opening (Fig. 126).

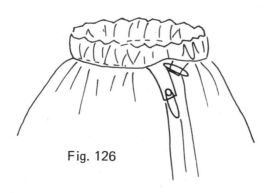

Fig. 126

Lap the ends of the elastic about 1 inch, pin, and try on for fit. Tighten if necessary. Overcast the edges of the elastic together (Fig. 127). Slip the elastic back inside, and stitch up the opening.

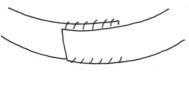

Fig. 127

Turn up the hem to the correct length. Measure in several places and pin (Fig. 128). Hem by hand, or instead, you can pin rickrack on the outside of the skirt, following the hemline (Fig. 129). Be sure to remove the pins from the under side before stitching. The hem will be stitched in place at the same time as the rickrack.

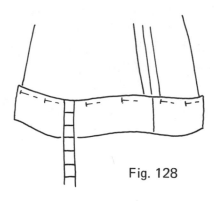

Fig. 128

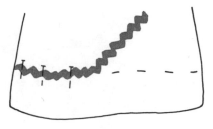

Fig. 129

A long *ankle-length skirt* for a small girl can be made the same way. For a bigger girl a fuller skirt is needed to allow room for walking.

Use two lengths of fabric, each about 30 inches wide, and have 2 seams, one on each side (Fig. 130).

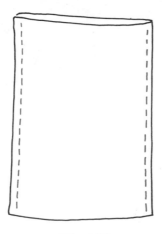

Fig. 130

A *wrap-around skirt* can be made with no seam at all. Finish the two opening edges with a narrow hem, then finish the top and bottom in the same way as the other skirt, but use a long piece of white cable cord instead of elastic, to run through the top and tie in a bow.

The skirt is worn with the opening at the side or the front, over a bathing suit or matching shorts.

Pants in a variety of lengths are very popular with girls, and are not hard to make, though this is one item that does require a pattern. A simple two-piece pattern with an elastic waist can be managed without much difficulty. Once you have learned the method by making one pair, you can keep turning them out like an assembly line!

All lengths of pants—shorts, long pants, knickers, or gauchos—are made exactly the same way. Often you can find several styles in one pattern. Choose the correct size by your hip measurement.

Check the length of long pants by holding the pattern up to your figure. You may have to add a little at the bottom if you are tall for your size.

The pattern instruction sheet will show the two pattern pieces arranged something like this (Fig. 131). Place them on your fabric, which is folded lengthwise, the way it usually comes from the store. The finished edges opposite the fold are called the *selvages*.

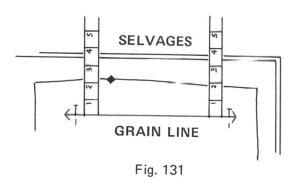

Fig. 131

Notice that each pattern piece has printed on it a long straight line with an arrow at either end. This is called the *grain line*, and must always be placed so that it is parallel to the selvages of the fabric. That is, both ends of the line must measure an equal distance from the edge. Check this with a ruler and pin at both ends (Fig. 132). If you neglect to do this, the pants or whatever you are making will come out crooked and twisted.

SELVAGES

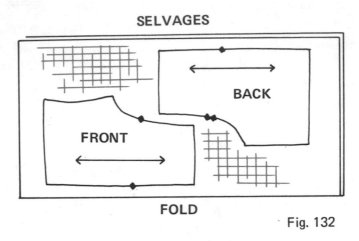

FOLD

Fig. 132

Finish pinning around the edges of the pattern pieces, and cut out.

There are three sets of seams in pants:

1. *The crotch seam*

Place the two fronts with right sides together, and pin along the curved crotch seam (Fig. 133).

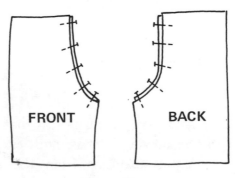

Fig. 133

Pin the two backs together the same way.

Stitch each seam ⅝ inch wide. (This is the standard seam width on all patterns.) Stitch the curved part of the seam a second time for extra strength (Fig. 134).

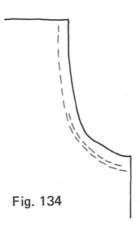

Fig. 134

Clip the curved part of the seam at intervals of ½ inch, almost up to the stitching (Fig. 135). Press both seams open.

Fig. 135

2.   *The side seams*

Place the front and back sections of the pants with right sides together, pin and stitch the two side seams (Fig. 136). (You will notice that the back of the pants is wider than the front. Don't be bothered by this—just be sure the edges match.)

Press the two seams open.

3.   *Last comes the inside leg seam*

Bring the ends of the two crotch seams together and pin. Continue pinning the full length of the legs. Stitch in one continuous seam from the bottom of one leg, across the crotch seam, and down to the bottom of the other leg (Fig. 137). Press the seam open, using a small sleeve board.

The elastic waist and the hems at the bottom of the legs can be finished the same way as the skirt.

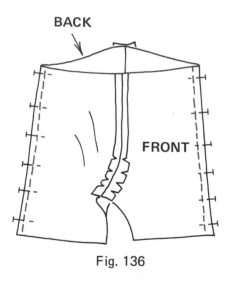

BACK

FRONT

Fig. 136

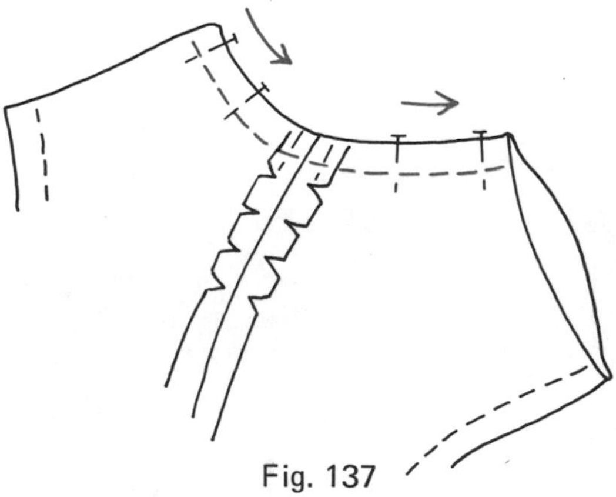

Fig. 137

This simple *popover top* can be made in a short length to wear over pants, a bit longer for a cover-all smock, or ankle length for a beach cover-up.

Make a pattern of wrapping paper. First, measure yourself around the widest part of your hips. Divide this figure by 2, and add 3 inches for a seam allowance and extra ease.

For instance, if you measure 30 inches, divide by 2 and get 15, add 3 inches for a total of 18 inches. This is the width of your pattern.

Follow the diagram in Fig. 138.

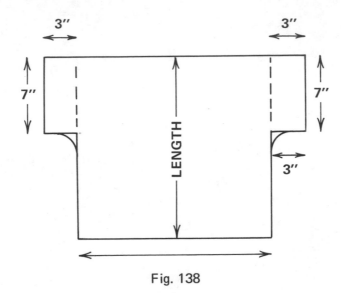

Fig. 138

Make a rectangle 18 inches wide, and the length measured from the top of your shoulder to the hem, plus 2 inches.

Add sleeves by measuring 3 inches out from each side, and 7 inches down from the top (8 inches in larger sizes). Draw a curved line for the underarm.

Pin the pattern to a double piece of fabric, with the right sides together. The top shown in the photo has a border print, and was placed crosswise on the fabric, with the selvages at the bottom edge. (In this case, no hem is needed.)

Cut out, pin the two side and underarm seams, and stitch ½ inch from the edge. Stitch twice over the underarm curve (Fig. 139).

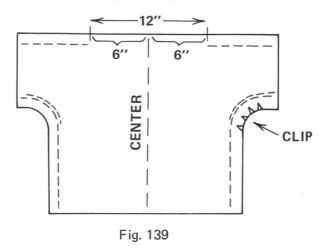

Fig. 139

For the neck opening, mark the center of the top edge, mark with a pin 6 inches from each side of the center, and stitch the shoulder seam from this point to the end of the sleeve, in a 1 inch seam.

Clip the underarm seams, and press all seams open. Continue to press under 1 inch at the neck edge. Turn under the raw edges of the neck, pin, and hem by hand (Fig. 140).

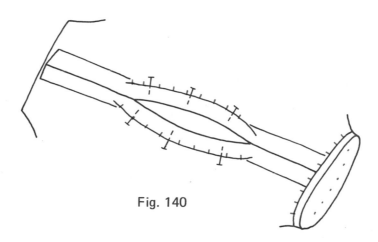

Fig. 140

Make a narrow hem on the sleeves.

The top shown here has ball fringe stitched to the lower edge. Make a plain hem if you do not use trimming.

The *long beach robe* version should be slit a few inches up the sides to allow room for walking (Fig. 141). Make a narrow hem on the side slits before finishing the bottom hem.

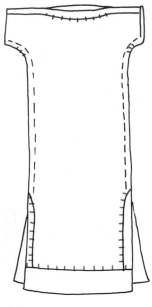

Fig. 141

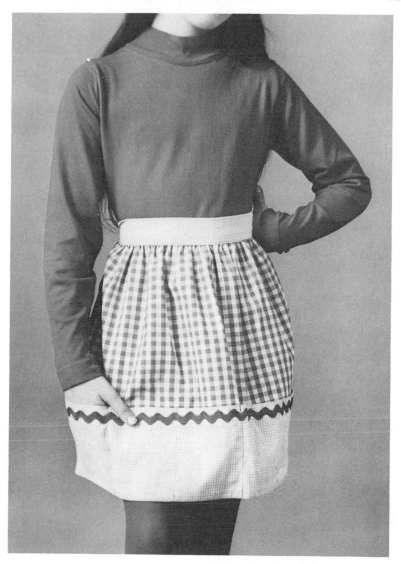

Make yourself an *apron* if you like to cook, or work with messy paints or clay.

This child's-size apron is made of a piece of fabric 24 inches wide and 14½ inches long. The large pocket is 24 inches by 6½ inches.

For the long pocket, press under ¼ inch on the top edge, then another ¾ inch. Pin rickrack on the outside, along the hem edge, and stitch (Fig. 142).

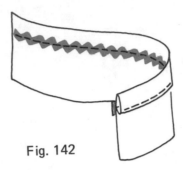

Fig. 142

On both side edges of the apron, make a small clip ½ inch deep, 4 inches up from the bottom. Turn under and stitch a narrow hem above the clip (Fig. 143).

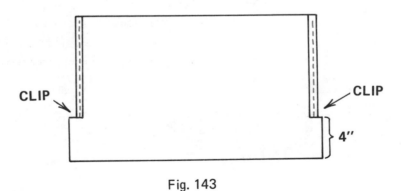

CLIP   CLIP

4"

Fig. 143

Stitch the *right* side of the bottom edge of the pocket to the *wrong* side of the bottom of the apron, in a ½-inch seam (Fig. 144). Turn the pocket up and press the seam flat. (The seam is now concealed inside the pocket.)

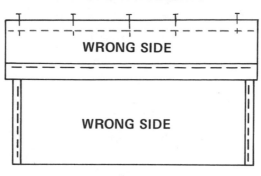

Fig. 144

Press under ½ inch on the ends of the pocket and the remaining raw edges of the apron (Fig. 145). Turn the

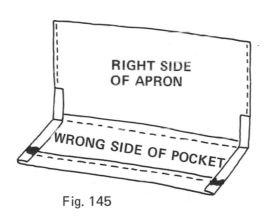

Fig. 145

pocket up, pin and top stitch both ends close to the edge (Fig. 146). Divide pocket into 4 or 5 equal sections by marking with chalk. Stitch over lines, backstitching firmly at top and bottom (Fig. 146).

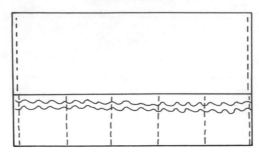

Fig. 146

Mark the center of the top edge by folding in half and making a small clip in the edge. Gather the top edge by making two rows of machine basting, the first ½ inch from the top, the second row just above it. Leave a few inches of thread at each end.

Gather by pulling up the underneath threads. First pull up one end until some gathers form, and wind the threads around a pin (Fig. 147a). Pull up the threads at the other end until the gathered edge measures 12 inches, and fasten the threads around another pin (Fig. 147b).

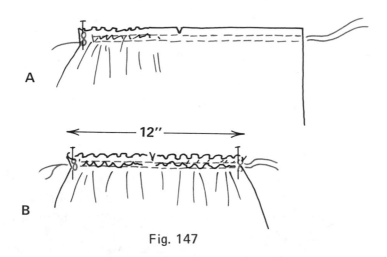

Fig. 147

For the waistband and ties, cut a strip of cloth about 58 inches long (this may be pieced) by 4 inches wide.

Mark the center of the band, and pin it to the center of the gathered edge, with right sides together and edges matching (Fig. 148). Pin the band along the whole gathered edge and stitch along the lower gathering thread.

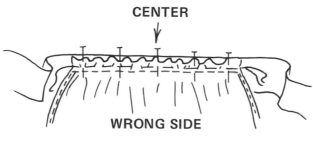

Fig. 148

Turn the band up, and fold the ends in half lengthwise, wrong side out (Fig. 149). Pin and stitch both tie ends in a ½-inch seam, stitching across the short ends, and stopping the stitching at the end of the gathered section.

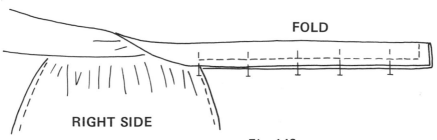

Fig. 149

Trim the seam, turn right side out, and press. (See directions for belt in Chapter Three.)

Turn under ½ inch on the inside of the waistband, pin, and hem invisibly in place (Fig. 150).

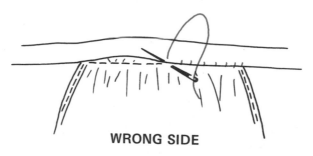

WRONG SIDE

Fig. 150

The same style can be made in an adult-size apron. Make it about 30 to 32 inches wide, 18 inches long, and the pocket section 8 to 10 inches deep. The ties can be a few inches longer.

Aprons can also be made with a plain stitched hem at the bottom, and trimmed in various ways. You can get ideas for trimming from other sections of this book, using braid, embroidery, or appliqué designs. Try a cross-stitch border on gingham, as described in Chapter Two.

CHAPTER SEVEN

DOLLS' CLOTHES

THIS CHAPTER gives you several basic patterns that will fit the standard 11½-inch teen doll. There are many different dolls of this type: Barbie, Dollikin, Francie, Maddie Mod, and numerous others.

The first thing to bear in mind is that such tiny clothes can be difficult to work on unless the proper materials are chosen. Anything that frays easily should be avoided.

Felt is especially good, as the edges need no finishing at all. Use it for coats, skirts, jackets, hats, or handbags.

Knit materials are especially good if they are not too heavy. Discarded socks or panty hose can be used.

Lightweight cottons can be used if they are firm and closely woven. Choose plain colors or very small patterns that will be in good proportion to the size of the doll.

For trimming, collect odds and ends of very small rickrack, lace, etc. Have some buttons and snaps in the smallest sizes.

If you make separate skirts, blouses, coats, pants, etc., in co-ordinated colors and materials, the parts can be switched around to make several different outfits.

First try several pieces in felt. A semi-circle *wrap-around skirt* has no seams at all.

Trace the pattern in Fig. 151 onto thin paper, cut out, and pin to a piece of felt. Cut out the skirt, wrap it around the doll with the opening at the left side, adjust to fit, and mark with pins where the snaps will be placed. Sew the ball part of the snaps under the right front edge, and the other half of the snaps on the outside of the left side (Fig. 152). Sew buttons to the outside, on top of the snaps.

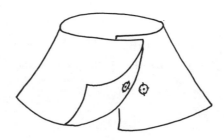

Fig. 152

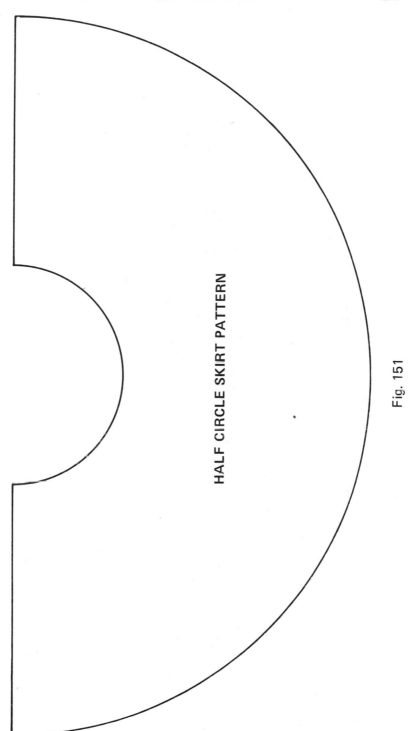

HALF CIRCLE SKIRT PATTERN

Fig. 151

Make a *matching coat* with the pattern in Figs. 153 and 154. Trace and cut out the patterns, pin the front on a double layer of felt, and cut out. Place the pattern for the back on a folded piece of felt, with the center back edge exactly in the fold, pin and cut out. Do *not* cut along the fold.

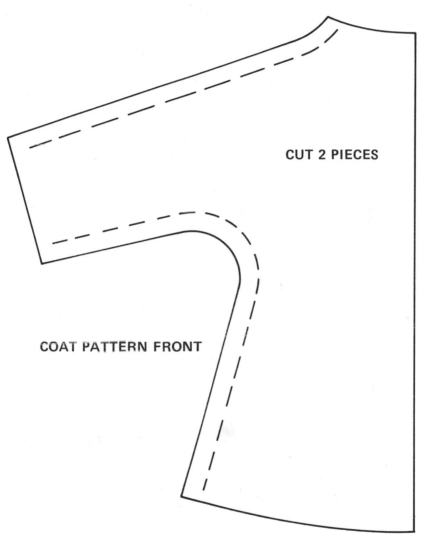

CUT 2 PIECES

COAT PATTERN FRONT

Fig. 153

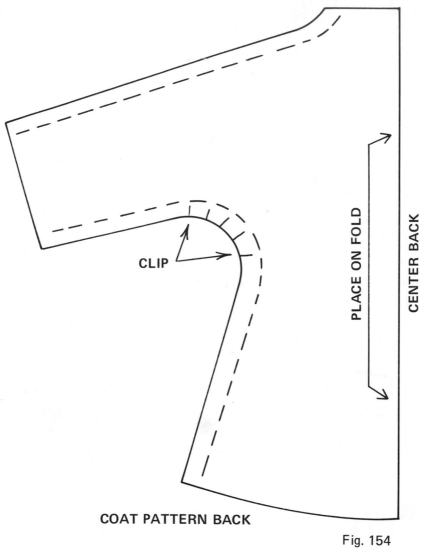

CLIP

PLACE ON FOLD

CENTER BACK

COAT PATTERN BACK

Fig. 154

Pin and stitch the sides and top of the sleeves (Fig. 155). The seam allowance on all these doll patterns is ¼ inch. You may stitch dolls' clothes on the machine, or do it by hand, using a backstitch. As dolls' clothes are so small, it is often easier to sew them by hand.

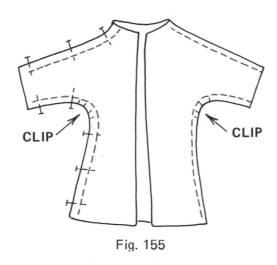

Fig. 155

Make several clips in the underarm seam, and turn the coat right side out. Sew three snaps to the front edges and sew a button on top of each snap.

A belt can be made of a strip of felt ½ inch wide and 9½ inches long. First make several rows of stitching close together on a wider piece of felt, then trim close to the stitching (Fig. 156). The belt is lapped over once and tied around the waist.

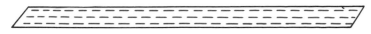

Fig. 156

A *sleeveless vest* is also made of felt, and is cut in one piece (Fig. 157). Place the center back line of the pattern on a fold of felt, pin and cut. Lap the shoulder seams

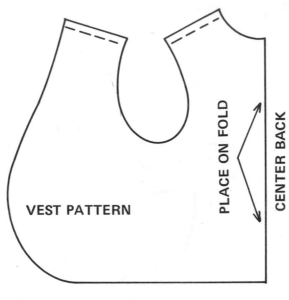

VEST PATTERN   PLACE ON FOLD   CENTER BACK

Fig. 157

from back to front ¼ inch and sew through the middle of the lapped sections (Fig. 158).

The front may be trimmed with embroidery or braid. (See Chapter Two.)

Fig. 158

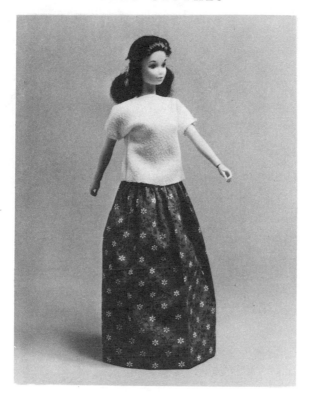

Another kind of *skirt* is made of a straight piece of fabric, gathered at the waist. This long version is made of a small patterned cotton. Cut a piece 12 inches wide and 7½ inches long. Fold in half, right sides together, and stitch the center back seam, leaving 1 inch open at the top (Fig. 159).

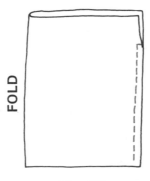

Fig. 159

Stitch two rows of machine basting around the top, pull up the ends of the thread to gather the skirt, and try it on the doll. Adjust for a snug fit, allowing ½-inch overlap at the waist, and tie the threads at both ends (Fig. 160).

Fig. 160

A piece of ribbon or seam binding is stitched to the outside of the gathers for a belt (Fig. 161). Turn under ¼ inch on one edge, sew a snap under it, and the other half of the snap on the opposite edge (Fig. 162).

Turn up the bottom to the correct length and hem. The bottom of the skirt may be trimmed with braid or embroidery.

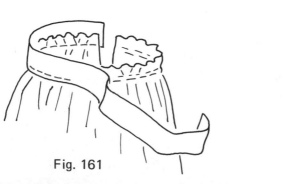

Fig. 161

Fig. 162

This pattern (Figs. 163 and 164) can be used for a *dress*, or for a blouse by cutting off at the short length. Sleeves can be long or short.

Pin the front of the pattern with the center line on a lengthwise fold, and cut out. Cut two pieces for the back.

With right sides together, stitch the center back seam to within 2 inches of the top. (Leave it open for the blouse.)

Trimming on the front should be added before the seams are stitched. This one has tiny white rickrack stitched along the center front.

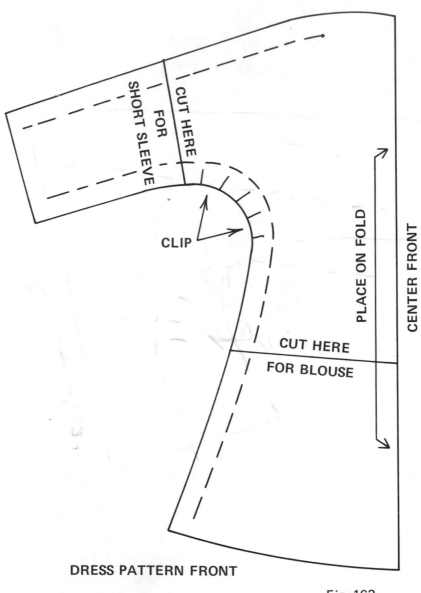

DRESS PATTERN FRONT

Fig. 163

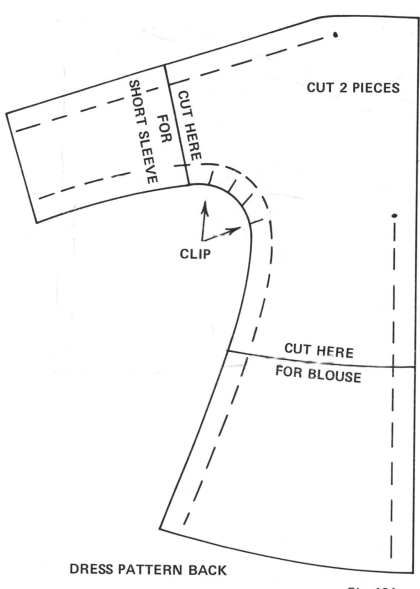

CUT 2 PIECES

CUT HERE

FOR
SHORT SLEEVE

CLIP

CUT HERE

FOR BLOUSE

DRESS PATTERN BACK

Fig. 164

With right sides together, stitch the two side underarm seams, and clip the curve under the arm (Fig. 165). Stitch the top of the shoulder and sleeve, ending the stitching at the point marked on the pattern.

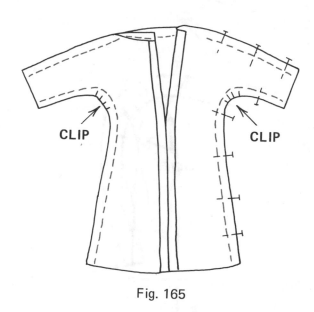

Fig. 165

Turn down the neck edge and sew by hand. Turn up and hem the sleeves and bottom edge. Turn right side out, turn under one opening edge, and fasten the back with snaps. Another strip of rickrack is used as a belt.

The *white knit blouse* shown with the skirts is made with short sleeves. The back is left open, and fastened with two snaps. It can be worn with either skirt, or the checked pants, and the vest can go over it.

The *pants pattern* (Fig. 166) is shown here made of checked gingham. Cut two pieces by the pattern, and stitch the two side seams, leaving one side open 1 inch from the top. Stitch the inside leg seams, and clip the curve between the legs (Fig. 167).

PANTS PATTERN

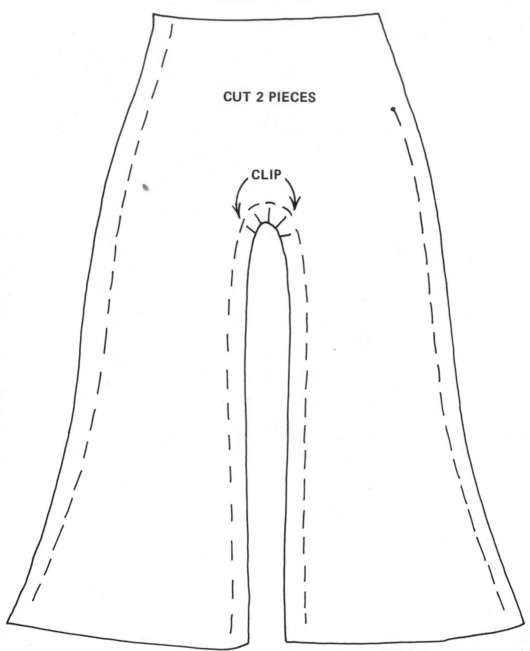

CUT 2 PIECES

CLIP

Fig. 166

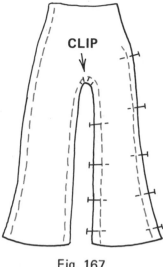

CLIP

Fig. 167

Turn down a narrow hem at the top, and hem the bottom of the legs.

Turn right side out, and fasten the waist with a snap on the left side.

A *matching poncho* is made of checked gingham, and can also be worn over the bathing suit.

Cut two by Fig. 168, keeping the bottom edges on a straight edge of fabric, so it can be fringed.

Stitch the two shoulder seams, ending the stitching at the point marked. Turn under a hem at the neck, and sew by hand (Fig. 169).

Fringe the bottom edges for ⅜ inch.

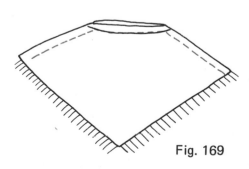

Fig. 169

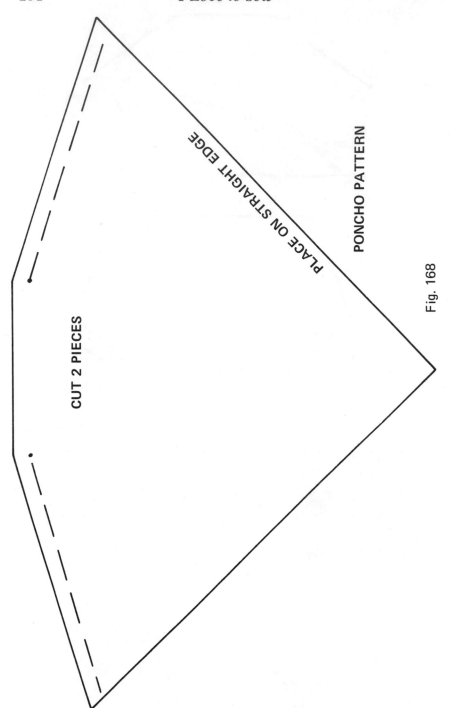

CUT 2 PIECES

PLACE ON STRAIGHT EDGE

PONCHO PATTERN

Fig. 168

Make the *bathing suit* (Fig. 170) of a firm knit that
will not fray. Place the pattern with the lower edge on a
fold, pin, and cut. With right sides together, stitch the
two side seams (Fig. 171). With a stretchy fabric, the
pants can be put on without any waist opening.

This pattern could also be used for underwear. Use discarded nylon tricot slips or pants, and trim the bottom
edges with narrow lace (Fig. 172).

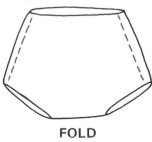

FOLD

Fig. 171

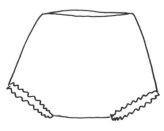

Fig. 172

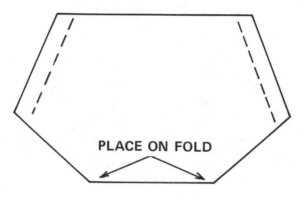

BATHING SUIT HALTER

PLACE ON FOLD

BATHING SUIT PANTS

Fig. 170

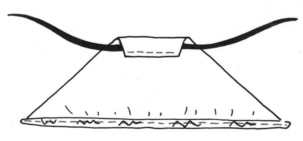

Fig. 173

Cut out the *halter*, turn up a narrow hem at the lower edge, and sew with a running stitch, gathering it slightly until it fits the doll (Fig. 173).

Turn down the top over a thin piece of cord or yarn, and sew the edge.

Fasten the two points with a snap at the back, and tie the cord around the neck.

A *nightgown* is made of two pieces of light cotton material, 9 inches long and 5½ inches wide.

Stitch the two side seams, leaving 1½ inches open at the top for armholes (Fig. 174). Turn under ¼ inch at the armholes and hem (Fig. 175).

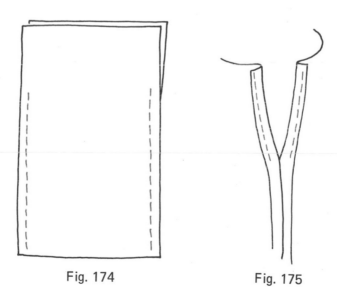

Fig. 174   Fig. 175

Turn under ½ inch at the top and make two rows of machine basting (Fig. 176). Pull up the gathers to fit the

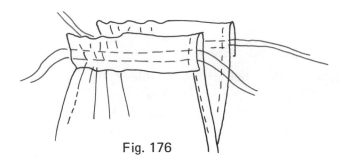

Fig. 176

doll's neck loosely, and tie the threads. Tie one armhole together at the top (Fig. 177), and leave the other open.

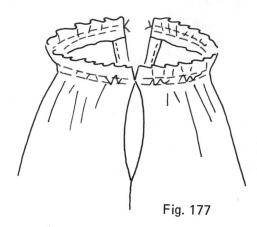

Fig. 177

Stitch a second time on top of the gathers, with a small stitch, to hold the gathers in place.

Turn up a hem, and sew narrow lace on the bottom. A zigzag stitch may be used if you have it (Fig. 178). Fasten the shoulder with a snap on the inside (Fig. 179).

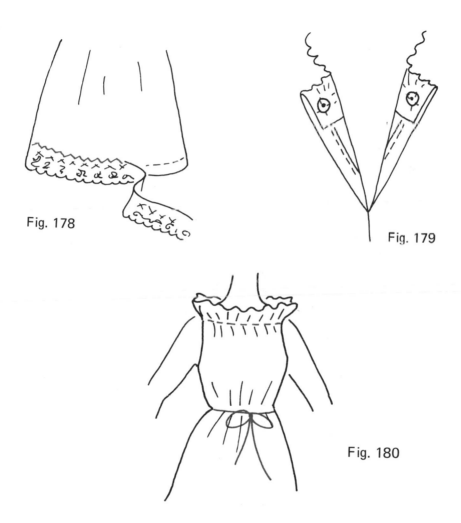

Fig. 178

Fig. 179

Fig. 180

Tie a narrow tape or ribbon at the waist (Fig. 180).

This could also be made in a short length, as a summer dress.

BARBARA CORRIGAN loves to sew. In fact, she's been sewing since childhood and now teaches sewing to adults and children as well as being a professional dressmaker and designer. Ms. Corrigan, who has lived in Attleboro, Massachusetts, all her life, graduated from the Massachusetts College of Art in 1944 and worked for many years as a freelance designer and illustrator for books, advertising, and greeting cards. She is also the author of another book on sewing, *Of Course You Can Sew*.